Haiku Heartsong

In Tribute to My Seeing Eye® Dogs

Rebecca Lineberger, Ph.D.

Haiku Heartsong
In Tribute to My Seeing Eye® Dogs
By Rebecca Lineberger, Ph.D.

Copyright © 2021 Rebecca Lineberger
All rights reserved.
Printed in the United States of America.

ISBN: 978-0-9841982-8-3

No part of this book may be used or reproduced or transmitted in any form or by any means, graphic, electronic or mechanical, including photocopying, scanning, recording, taping, internet, or by any information storage and retrieval systems, without written permission of the publisher or author.

Published by:
Off The Leash Press, LLC
Winter Park, FL 32789
offtheleashpress.com
info@offtheleashpress.com
407-758-8309

Editing, Interior Layout, Consultation Services, and Cover Design:
Off The Leash Press, LLC

Front cover photograph of Eagle in harness and interior photograph of Trek in harness - Courtesy of:

The Seeing Eye, Inc.
P.O. Box 375
Morristown, NJ 07963
SeeingEye.org

Library of Congress Control Number: 2021909744

For my guides, journeys may end,

but never my gratitude.

Contents

About The Seeing Eye vii
Author's Note ix
Forward xi
My Dogs 1
Minx 3
Tosca 45
Daphne 87
Eagle 129
Afterward 171
Postscript 177
About the Author 183

About The Seeing Eye

"Seeing Eye® is a registered trademark for guide dogs of The Seeing Eye, Inc., and is its registered service mark for training dogs as guides and instructing visually impaired individuals in their use and care."

"The mission of The Seeing Eye is to enhance the independence, dignity and self-confidence of people who are blind, through the use of specially trained Seeing Eye dogs."

For more information, visit SeeingEye.org.

Author's Note

Wiktionary says that "heartsong" is obsolete. So be it, but the word is just right, so I'm keeping it!

1. A heartwarming song or poem.
2. A song or message that is deeply heartfelt.
3. The expression of a person's inner essence, underlying identity, and reason for existence.

Any or all of the above.

Forward

So Much to Tell

Words into stories,
what to say, how to say it.
Add, cut. Make them fit.

Come Walk a While with Me

Journeys begin and end. Who we walk with can make all the difference.

My Dogs

Minx: a female yellow Labrador retriever
Tosca: a female yellow Labrador retriever
Daphne: a female yellow Labrador/golden retriever cross
Eagle: a male yellow Labrador retriever

Minx

In the Beginning, A Guide's Lament

"I told you to stop!

Why don't you pay attention?"

Loud Labrador sigh.

Trusting Your Dog

Snow. Curbs disappear.

"Where are we?" "I know —" "I'll ask."

"He's wrong!" And he was!

Intelligent Disobedience

"Minx, forward." "No." Tape across the sidewalk — is there a hole — yes! "Good girl!"

Joined

It's just a handle,

but oh, what joy it can bring!

Four paws, two feet. Free!

Housemates, Working It Out

"I was here first," said Damsel with feline logic.

"She needs me. Adjust!"

Cats!

"Purr. See me on her bed?" "Minx, come." "Have a nice nap. I have things to do!"

She left it!

The cat's bowl is clean.

Labrador looking guilty?

"Who me?" Cat says, "Yes!"

Other Plans

Restaurant dining.

Following our friend, I thought.

Laughter. Kitchen bound!

Season's Change

Southward Canada
geese fly. Labrador fur grows
winter-thick again.

My Guide at Play

"Snowflakes on my nose!

Chase them, taste them, pounce, dive, roll.

Warm you with my joy!"

Dining Out, Almost

"What may I bring her? Water, a bit of steak?" "Yes, please!" "No. She's working."

Together, Running Free
(Colorado, The Great Sand Dunes National Park)

"Want to come with me?"

"Let's go!" Fast, faster. Running!

Two as one! Pure joy!

Abundance

Fur, fur, everywhere!
I brush and brush, yet always
you have more to share.

On Watch

In church early. Dark.

Shadows of monks filing in.

Low growl, "Who are you?"

Your Name for All to See

In school together.

My dissertation, your name.

"For guidance given …"

Encounter with an Ocean

"Let's get our feet wet."

"No way. My job is to keep you safe. That thing roars!"

Rescued

In the pool, hoping to swim. "I'll save you!" Splash, Minx nudging, "Not far now …"

Art Festival in the Park, Taking a Break

We sit on the grass.

A sign says, "No Dogs Allowed!"

Policeman looks, leaves.

Full Circle

I carry you up

and down steps you can't walk now.

Taking care of you.

Love's Last Gift

Lying beside you,
holding you, letting you go.
No more pain. Peace, joy.

Tosca

Training, Starting Over

"Follow your dog. Pay attention." Learning to read all over again.

Canine Logic

Walking 'round puddles,

you keep *your* feet dry, not mine!

"Snort! *You* have boots on!"

Waterlogged

Not just rain — buckets

of rain — torrents of rain! Miles

yet to go. Splash on.

Doubly Careful

Making sure I stop,
you don't just show me the curb.
You turn, block my way.

Always Ask

"Do you need help?" "No, thank you. I have my dog. But thank you for asking."

Joy in Showing Me

Paws on the mailbox,

on the bar of a glass door.

"It's here, see?" "Good girl!"

In Her Vet's Waiting Room

"What a beautiful
dog! And so well-mannered too."
Tosca smiles. Me too.

Paying Taxes, A long Memory

"No, my desk is here."

"But last year?" "Oh my! Yes, there. And she remembered!"

Blue Jays! Why Won't You Listen?

"Stop! Your nest is safe. We're just passing through. Can't you see that I'm working?"

Caught in the Act

"Where's my Tosca?" "Oops! Quick — Phew!" "The sofa is warm where you were lying."

Woof! What was that?

Blankets on the grass.

Christmas music in the air.

Camel walking by.

Christmas Temptation

You're home by yourself.

A gift left on the sofa.

For you? Why not check …

Where Are His People?

"Loose dog underfoot as I try to guide. Does no one care about him?"

Just for You!

Carrots from my hand.

"Yes, but I want them sliced, please."

"Certainly, ma'am." "Crunch!"

Perks of My Job

"Pet dogs underneath tables outside. All watch me as we go inside."

Feline Power Play

"Growl. Pass if you dare!"

"There's a cat. Shall I move her?"

Hands reach. Tosca smiles.

A Standing Ovation
(Bach Festival Concert)

Paws on back of pew.

Tail waving, "Encore! Encore!"

Applause and laughter.

Tail Talk

"Thump, thump! Here I am!
Hear my tail? Did you want me?
See me. I'm right here!"

For Your Ears Only

You on the sofa,

me on the floor. Rub your soft

ears. Whisper your name.

Career Change, More Yet to Do

From one step to the

next, something's wrong! Not paws ... hip?

A new job. Kids smile.

Daphne

Yet Another Beginning

Oh my! So tiny.

Only forty-seven pounds!

My goldador girl.

Places to Go

"Daffers? Daffodil?"

"Yes?" Your plumed tail brushes my wrist. Paws dance. "Where next?"

The Magic Word

Your head on my foot,

under my desk as I work.

Soft snores. Whisper, "Walk?"

Cookies

Allergies galore.

Shots to keep you well. Cookies

for your vet. "Thank you!"

Miles Together

"Forward … left … right …" through
a maze of turns we choose, till
our route brings us home.

Coming Home

Long walk. "We're almost home." "Wag," you say. "Boom! Boom!" The Shuttle says, "Me too!"

Unspoken Warning?

"There's a rabbit by

the path," our friend says. Daphne

looks, "Beware that hawk."

The Cinnamon Caper

Hot cornbread cooling.
"Cinnamon! Just one small bite —
Yum!" Clink. "Oh no! Caught!"

Confusion

"But why can't I eat
the toothbrush? It's in my mouth.
You gave it ... took it ..."

A Guide's "Tail" of Woe

"Shoppers look, but not where they put their feet! Oh, the tales our tails could tell!"

Road Hogs

"Hugging the edge of
the road. No sidewalk. Watching.
Cars don't always look!"

Swimming

Walking by the pool.

Splash, splash. Me, "Are they nuts? It's cold!" You, "Wag, just ducks!"

Weather Woes

"You don't like thunder. What about hurricanes?" "I don't like those either!"

Playing Tug with You

"See how strong I am?"

"You just showed me! But also,

'Drop it,' how gentle."

Making Allowances

"He's chewing my ears!
He's chewing my tail! Patience.
He's just a puppy."

A New Toy

They said this one would

be "chew-proof." But they forgot

to test it on you!

Clippers

"I love my vet. She
can poke and prod, I don't mind.
But trim my nails — No!"

"Again?"

"Here's my Kong. Throw please?"

Toss high. Leap! "Caught it!" "Good girl!"

"Here's my Kong. Throw please …"

Tummy Rubs

Eyes closed, blissed out. "There, and there…" Paws grab my hand. "Yes! Just there — My ears too?"

Time to go

Surrounded by those

who love you. Saying good-bye.

Brush of angel's wings.

Eagle

Getting Acquainted, Saying "Well Done"

Click, treat. "No thank you. I don't take food from strangers."

"A hug instead?" "Wag."

"What a Wonderful Dog!"

Sidewalk sale. Tables piled high. Shoppers browsing, kids, dogs. You — Calm, focused.

"Haycorn" Hazard

Canopy of oaks

shade. Litter of acorns fall.

Paws careful. Feet too!

Your Gift to Me

Red-Shouldered Hawk in the park, an Eagle beside me. "Freedom — What joy!"

Teaching, Still Doors to Open

"You can't bring that dog inside." "Yes. He's a Seeing Eye dog." "Oh. Okay."

Hunger Pangs

Nose touching my hand.
"Eleven o'clock. Snack please.
Yes, now! Crunch, gulp. More?"

The Great Escape

"Where's my toy? I can't find it!" "Is this it?" "Yes! But who took it outside?"

Making Me Smile

Lying on your back,

holding your Kong in your paws.

Tasting contentment.

At the Mall

"So much to see — What
are those dark squares on the floor?
Holes? Go around them!"

Reassuring Touch

Heeling through the store. Quick kiss to my hand on the cart. "Hello, I'm here …"

A Matter of Opinion

"Singing? Some think so.

Back row. Still too loud. Advice?

Howl more softly, please."

Tooth Extraction, Taking Antibiotics

"Pill pockets — I don't think so! I saw that nasty pill you put inside!"

Greetings

Sandhill Cranes watch from the grass as we walk by. No one speaks. Just a nod.

Meeting a Turtle

"Strange beast in our way.
Sniff, sniff. I can't stop now, but
I'll know you next time!"

Grooming Interruption

Ground shakes. Distant roar. Brush pauses. "Don't stop! Just the Shuttle leaving Earth."

Snake Etiquette

"Stop! Now!" "What is it?"
"I don't like him!" Slither, slide.
"Forward?" "Not yet — Now."

Early Morning Conversation

Sun not yet awake.

"Who, who-who?" Just a Barred Owl,

my Eagle and me.

Heartsong

Your heart is broken,

they tell me. And yet your love

flows strong with each beat.

Your Work Done

Taking care of me.

Gentle, calm, eyes filled with love.

"Thank you! Go in peace."

Missing You

Harness on its peg,

all toys neatly in their box.

But my guide — is gone.

Afterward

My Heart Says

"To love and to serve,
a guide dog's gift." Some would say
not, but they'd be wrong!

Who First Named Them "Dog"? Love, Surely

From left to right, "dog."

But switch them 'round, "god." That "o,"

linking, "we're all one."

Postscript

"Hello! My name is Trek!"

"Woof! I've just met my forever person. Someone special who needs me!"

With You by My Side, All Things are Possible

New places to go,

new people to meet. Today,

our journey begins.

About the Author

Rebecca Lineberger has always loved dogs. But they could never come with her everywhere she went. Time eventually exchanged sight for insight, and four wonderful Seeing Eye® dogs came into her life. They earned a Ph.D. together, she and Minx, just because Rebecca loved books, and because Minx loved Rebecca. Then they went forth into the wide world to have adventures. Not as many, nor as exciting as Bilbo's, but adventures all the same.

Now, half a human lifetime later — days and days of living and loving — how to summarize that joy of working and playing together, and eventually, the heartbreak of having to say good-bye. For Rebecca, these haiku were her answer, her way of healing after she lost her beloved Eagle. But as three times before, out of sadness comes joy, with the beginning of yet another journey with her fifth dog, and still more adventures waiting for them to share.

It is her hope that anyone who has been blessed by the love of a dog will find love and laughter, and healing too, in these haiku journeys. They are truly songs from the heart.

www.ingramcontent.com/pod-product-compliance
Lightning Source LLC
Chambersburg PA
CBHW051944290426
44110CB00015B/2106